FuzzBall

Ben Newell

Fuzzball © 2019 by Ben Newell. Exterior copyright © 2019 by Julie Valin. All rights reserved. No part of this book may be used or reproduced in any manner whatsoever without written permission except in the case of brief quotations embedded in critical articles and reviews.

First edition. Printed in the USA.

ISBN: 978-1-926860-66-4

Some of these poems originally appeared in Chiron Review, The Dope Fiend Daily, 48th Street Press Broadside Series, HSTQ, LUMMOX, Midnight Lane Boutique, Nerve Cowboy, Pink Litter, Tree Killer Ink, and The Very Best of the Beatnik Cowboy.

Epic Rites Press publications are distributed worldwide by Tree Killer Ink. For more information about *Fuzzball* (and other books and publications from Epic Rites Press) please visit the Epic Rites website at www.epicrites.org.

Epic Rites: any press is only as "small" as its thinking

Contents

get this guy a sandwich 9
on the road to recovery 10
#1 doctor recommended brand 11
despondent 12
secret sauce 13
man's best friend 14
america's pastime 15
black pajamas 16
james patterson 17
chocolate decadence 18
old school 19
blowtorch 20
hidden gem 21
death of a sage 22
mikey likes it 23
fuzzball 24
take it to the hole 25
polly 26
first-person shooter 27
smile supplies 28
fresh meat 29
blackout 30
rejected by runner's world 31
remedy 32
another bodily fluid 33
the new yorker book of cat cartoons 34
jeopardy 35

mindless work	36
wants to date but nothing serious	37
flu season	38
late bloomer	39
wet dream	40
discreet billing	41
coffee and cookies and a lack of clarity	42
radioactive rainy day fund	43
funny no matter how you slice it	44
make check payable to	45
day job	46
day two of national poetry month	47
death knell	48
police brutality	49
code yellow	50
pieces of paper	51
gumshoe	52
regimen	53
cam 2 cam	54
fucked	55
let a stranger be your friend	56
permanent recall	57
plop	58

FuzzBall

Ben Newell

get this guy a sandwich

He deadens
the area with a needle,
cuts out the clot
and
plugs me with gauze;
the procedure
is extremely painful
yet short in duration;
before leaving
I ask him if it's okay
to run—
"Run? Man, you don't
need to run. You're
skinny enough…"
Then he addresses
his staff: "CAN SOME-
BODY GET THIS GUY
A SANDWICH? I'M
AFRAID HE'S GOING
TO BLOW AWAY!"
They all enjoy a good
laugh at my expense;
the distance runner is
an easy target, always
has been, always will
be
but this isn't a poem
about the plight of
the distance runner,
this is a poem about
two assholes.

on the road to recovery

Peer-reviewed
hemorrhoid literature
advises me
to remove all reading material
from the bathroom.

So I shift my crapper library
to the bedroom.

Each and every volume —

With the exception
of the Lindsay Lohan *Playboy*
I didn't buy
for the articles, anyway.

#1 doctor recommended brand

I think
I'm done.

Alcohol dehydrates
and
this causes constipation
which wreaks havoc
on hemorrhoids.

A $400 procedure
involving a needle
and scalpel
has sobered my ass up.

My new drink of choice —

A tall glass of water
mixed with 2 rounded teaspoons
of Metamucil.

My poems
haven't really improved.

But my bunghole
is much better.

despondent

My first fulltime job
was working the circulation desk
at a public library.

One day
my boss called me into her office.

"I'm concerned," she said. "Quite frankly,
we all are. You seem so despondent."

It doesn't say much for my vocabulary
but I didn't know what that meant—

After our meeting
I went straight to the reference section
and consulted a thesaurus [a homeless man
had recently smuggled our dictionary
into the restroom
and smeared it with feces].

despondent, *adj.* downcast, melancholy,
depressed, dejected, disconsolate, wretched…

I hated like hell to admit it
but for once
that bitch was right.

secret sauce

The tall line cook
with impossibly tight apple ass
wants wings.

But we don't have wings
on our menu
so she places an order via smart phone
to be delivered
to the service entrance.

"This place has the best wings,"
she says. "The secret is in the sauce…"

I load
a rack of glasses into the dish machine
and think about it —

The tall line cook
with impossibly tight apple ass
down on her knees.

My secret spattered all over
her face.

man's best friend

I'm reading
Dean Koontz's *Watchers*.

One of the main characters
is a genetically engineered dog
capable of astonishing feats.

Such as
fetching icy cold cans of Coors
from the fridge
and delivering them to its master.

Some pooch —

A dog like that
would've made Bukowski
kick his fucking cats
to the curb.

america's pastime

I asked her
if she would stick a finger
in my ass
while I jerked off—

"Okay," she said, "but I want
to wear a glove…"

All I had in my apt.
was an old baseball mitt.

So we just said
fuck it
and played catch.

black pajamas

As a kid
in the early 80s
I went trick-or-treating
wearing a pair of
black pajamas.

Kung fu bad ass —

Unfortunately
I was struck by a car.

Not because
the driver
couldn't see me.

But because
the driver
was a Vietnam vet
with PTSD.

james patterson

The heavily tattooed
ex-gangbanger line cook
didn't learn
how to read until he was 20.

"I learned in prison," he says.

Then, "Better late than never…"

"You're absolutely right," I say.

And I don't bust his balls
for liking James Patterson.

I'm the dishwasher
but
I'm not stupid.

chocolate decadence

The heavily tattooed
ex-gangbanger line cook
comes back to the dish pit
with his smart phone.

Shows me pics
of all the wonderful dishes
he prepares at home.

Juicy
porterhouse steaks.

Taco platters heaped
with sour cream.

BBQ ribs slathered
with sauce—

Now he's showing me
some big-assed chick
twerking in his garage.

"Who's that?" I ask.

"That," he says, "is dessert."

old school

He called from San Antonio,
a skate punk pal from way back.

"Two hundred pounds," he said.
"Time to start exercising before
it's too late…"

A few days later
he texted me a pic of his new board —

This was two weeks ago
and I haven't heard from him since.

I figure he's in the zone
or
a full body cast.

blowtorch

Our hottest waitress
is having a bad day.

Big time slammed.

No relief in sight—

"When I get out of here,"
she says, "I'll definitely need
to work off some aggression."

I'd love
to help her with that
but lack the courage
to share this.

She's caramelizing
crème brulee
and I don't want to
get burned.

hidden gem

I'm looking at this chick
on the cover
of my contributor copy.

Pink lace panties
accentuating her stellar ass—

Who is this goddess?

The editor's girlfriend?

If so
he's one lucky bastard.

And determined, too.

No telling how much slush
he had to endure
to find a work of art like her.

death of a sage
for Liam

He told us
to avoid a major life decision
while attending
the intensive 10-day residency.

Don't call
your spouse demanding
a divorce.

This isn't real,
this is an alternate reality.

Wait until you return from
this boot camp for writers,
this controlled chaos,
this Vortex —

Sound advice he delivered
with authority
and much panache
and followed when he got back
to the city
and pulled the trigger.

mikey likes it

I'm walking along
when this hot brunette comes outside,
yelling as she crosses the street…

"MIKEY! MIKEY! MIKEY!"

She collars him in the neighbor's yard,
smacks him a good one
and tells him
to get his butt back to the house—

Despite the rather harsh reprimand
I wish I was Mikey
then I could lick my balls
when she takes off those yoga pants.

fuzzball

Just last night
I masturbated to a back issue
of *SWANK*.

1977
publication date.

The year *Star Wars*
was released.

A time
of widespread
sci-fi fever —

Surprisingly
none of the photos
had
a space opera theme.

Unless you count
the bountiful bush rivaling
that of Chewbacca's
fuck buddy.

take it to the hole

All of 18
our Saturday busboy
has managed
to get his girlfriend pregnant.

Fret not.

He has a plan.

It involves the installation
of a basketball goal
in his mother's driveway
where he can work on his game
en route to the NBA —

I'm surprised he was able
to get his girlfriend pregnant
in the first place.

With a plan like that
you'd think he would've tried
to stick it in her ear.

polly

I lived beneath her
in the basement apt.

The place was affordable
but
she was the real draw.

I had a serious hard-on
for my landlady —

In an attempt to impress
I raked the yard
on several occasions.

It was a big yard
with lots of trees
and a steep hill.

But it was
all for nothing.

The closest I came
to pussy
was feeding her cat.

first-person shooter

I feel sorry
for people who can't save it
for the page.

Letting the
disappointment, frustration, anger
accumulate
until the inevitable explosion.

You hear about it
all the time.

Somebody loses it
[usually at work]
and goes
on a killing spree.

If only they could save it
for the page—

Blasting out the lines,
a bloody massacre much cheaper
than the AK-47.

Or even
the Xbox 360.

smile supplies

I go to the dentist
for
my 6-month checkup.

No cavities,
no oral cancer,
no suspicious lumps
in my neck.

Myriad reasons
to smile.

Even
the little plastic bag
they give me
on my way out
reads
SMILE SUPPLIES—

In addition
to the ubiquitous toothbrush,
the little plastic bag
contains
a little tube of toothpaste,
a little spool of floss,
a little card reminding me
of my next appointment.

Everything so little.

Except the bill
which makes me
frown.

fresh meat

Our new line cook
plunges her hands
willy-nilly
into the sudsy depths.

Bad move.

I try to keep knives
out of my sink
but some of these retards
forget the rule—

I start to warn her
then decide against this.

I've always loved
slasher films.

The gorier,
the better.

blackout
for wolf

One of my favorite poets
prints poems
on the backs of unpaid bills.

I can see him now.

Hunched over a table,
pen in hand,
dashing off another gem.

Then everything goes black—

And he doesn't know
if it's the power company
or the tequila.

rejected by runner's world

I'm
pounding the pavement
when this young hottie
overtakes me.

And here
I had thought this
a pretty rapid clip —

Torn between shame
and elation.

Getting old
and slow sucks.

But that fleeting glimpse
of her tight ass
is the most excitement
I've had in months.

remedy

Driving home from work
when
I see the billboard.

Cartoonish illustration of some guy
sitting on the toilet,
face twisted with much pain
and strain.

NO GO IS NO GOOD —

I have no idea
if the stuff helps you shit
but the ad
definitely helped me overcome
a bad case of writer's block.

another bodily fluid

I had just
moved in to my new apt.

Boxes strewn all over
the place—

"Look, Mom," I said.
"This one is full of contributor copies."

"Wow," she said, "that represents a lot of
blood, sweat, and tears."

And another bodily fluid
I kept to myself
out of respect for her.

the new yorker book of cat cartoons

Mom orders this from Amazon,
an Xmas gift
for my brother's feline-loving fiancée.

Upon its arrival
she reads a few pieces
with much regret—

"I'm sending this back," she says.
"These don't even make sense."

"Think those are bad," I say,
"you should try their poetry…"

jeopardy

I finish my shift at the restaurant
then
return to my mother's house
to find her watching television.

Exquisite timing as Alex
launches a litany of literary questions.

"Beats! Harlem Renaissance! Steampunk!
Southern Gothic! Metafiction!"

It feels damn good
beating them to the buzzer,
besting today's assemblage
of intellectuals —

"Well," my mother says, "at least your
education wasn't a total waste…"

B.A., M.A., M.F.A.

46-year-old dishwasher
living at home.

For this
I have no answer.

mindless work

"Work smart,"
my late father said, "not hard."

Sorry, Dad, but I failed
to implement your advice.

I'm a dishwasher
earning $10.50 per hour—

$10.50 per plate
and I'd be a fucking genius.

Instead of
just another
scrub.

wants to date but nothing serious

I tried POF,
paid the fee, filled out my profile
and posted a pic.

Very little came of this.

One woman agreed to meet
for coffee
but I wound up cancelling
the date.

Sometimes you just know —

Of course
I won't be renewing my membership;
online dating
doesn't work for me.

I'm much better in the flesh,
out of the bushes
and from behind with a rag
soaked in chloroform.

flu season

He writes
in the waiting room,
writes
while his mother receives
medical care;
I hope he's aware
of the risks,
hope he keeps his hands
away from
contaminated magazines,
hope
he doesn't touch
his eyes, nose, mouth—
I'd hate for him to get
that kind of sick;
judging from his poetry
his mind
is already beyond repair.

late bloomer

The six-pack in my fridge
has been
there for a month.

Not even
the least bit tempting.

I guess this means
I'm not an alcoholic

Of course
there's still plenty of time—

At 46
I could be a late bloomer.

History supports this
as I didn't get laid until
I was 28.

Interestingly enough
she was an alcoholic
and extremely drunk.

wet dream

A few nights ago
I actually had one.

Rather disconcerting
for a man of my age.

That I'm currently living
with my mother
makes this even more unnerving.

What's next?

Acne?

A Ratt poster
taped to my bedroom wall?

Clandestine/late night viewings
of *Porky's*?

One thing's for certain —

This week
even if my mother insists
[and she often does]
I'll definitely
do my own laundry.

discreet billing

I've been
thinking about it for weeks
but
just can't find the courage
to ask for her number.

Not so much a lack of confidence in myself
as a lack of confidence
in her ability/willingness to overlook
my myriad flaws.

A 46-year-old dishwasher
living with his mother
isn't exactly a prize catch—

Also,
she works at the bank
and has unlimited access
to my financial records.

coffee and cookies and a lack of clarity

The old poet has returned
to his alma mater,
returned after a most lengthy absence
to serve
as some sort of scholar-in-residence.

Class of 1952,
the old poet then went on to Yale
where he earned his PhD —

Our boss forced us to have coffee and cookies
with the guy
in the employee lounge,
a party of sorts to make him feel welcome.

He ate more cookies than any of us
and talked a lot
but I couldn't decipher a word he said
and I didn't bother
with his poems,
figuring they would be even more
confusing.

radioactive rainy day fund

Enough with
the dramatic emails…

HELP KEEP THE ARTS ALIVE!
THE ARTS ARE BEING SLASHED!
THE ARTS ARE UNDER ATTACK!

Don't respond, don't make a tax-deductible
contribution via PayPal—

Disregard and delete,
save your money
for the post-apocalyptic brothel.

Tell the mutated whore
you work best under pressure
then ask her
if they have any openings.

funny no matter how you slice it

I'm reading *Deadly Thrills*,
an out of print paperback about
the Chicago Rippers,
a band of serial killers active in the early 80s;
Robin Gecht and his minions
trolled the Windy City in a Dodge van,
snatching women off the streets at will.

They liked to sever breasts
and use them for satanic sex play.

A harrowing tale,
certainly not the type to induce laughter
yet here I sit,
grinning and chuckling after reading
this—

"...small groups of detectives kept each other
abreast of the latest revelations..."

You have to question the author's word
choice;
all I can figure is she missed it
or perhaps her editor has a sense of humor
as sick as mine.

make check payable to

They encourage you to subscribe;
your support is vital,
your support helps them stay afloat;
this makes perfect sense
yet
creates a troubling dilemma:
are they publishing your poems
because they're good
or
because you're a loyal subscriber?
There's only one way to find out:
let your subscription expire,
wait a few months
then send them a fresh batch;
that's what I did —
A few weeks later
I received a form rejection letter
and
electric bill;
the rejection hurt like hell
but
at least I had the money to keep
the power on.

day job

I'm mopping the floor
when the sales rep shows up
to extol the superiority
of his employer's seafood.

My boss
stands there in his chef's jacket
listening patiently
to the well-rehearsed pitch.

The sales rep is still at it
when I dump the dirty mop water
and clock out—

Driving home,
I think about the fish sticks
in my freezer
and how even the best of us
have to do something else.

day two of national poetry month

Finds me
at the clinic.

Should I
start sobbing during today's session
there's a box of tissues
within easy reach.

I've been under psychiatric care
for 13 years
and haven't cried yet.

No need
in starting now —

Though I come damn close
an hour later.

Browsing exalted quarterlies
at Books-A-Million,
torturing myself with indecipherable verse,
already looking forward to next month.

Magnificent May,
the 5th to be exact
and my free comic book.

death knell

The director's lecture
was a programmatic requirement,
a source of much anguish
for many of us.

Sitting in that stifling auditorium,
listening to her go on
and on
and on
and on
in deadening monotone,
boring material delivered in her boring
manner—

"The alarm clock rang," she said.
"Never, ever, begin a piece…"

That hated voice still mocks me
as I reach for silence
with
trembling hand,
knocking the whole damn mechanism
to the floor…

AAA batteries spill out—

Guts from a suicide jumper who said
no
to another day, week, lecture
on opening lines
to avoid
but not a single word about
checking out with
the alarm clock rang.

police brutality

I'm watching an episode
of *Rookies*,
a reality series about cops
in training.

The jaded veteran
asks his young charge what he likes to do
in his spare time—

"Lift weights," the rookie says,
"and write poetry."

"What kind of poetry?"

"Love poetry."

I wince
and writhe in pain
and promptly change the channel.

code yellow

I'm watching
an episode of *Live PD*.

While being taken into custody
the subject shits in his pants.

Officers
call this "Code Brown" —

Years ago
I was the victim of a violent crime
which made me piss myself.

The guy didn't brandish a weapon,
didn't even demand money;
he just appeared in the stairwell
and started punching.

One of the most frightening
and
humiliating experiences of my life.

To this day
I regret not fighting back.

pieces of paper

The co-owner/chef
is out today,
attending class in order to renew
his ServSafe certificate.

The health dept.
requires this credential.

The health dept. doesn't require
my credential;
they don't give a flying fuck
about my MFA —

Nor does anybody else
for that matter.

I guess
that's why I'm the dishwasher.

gumshoe

She taught English
at this city's premier prep school.

I don't know the story
but now she's waiting tables
here
where I wash dishes.

Presently scooping ice cream
to top off
a customer's pie —

"Jeez," she says, "this stuff is
hard as a rock…"

Hard as a rock.

Such clichéd language
for one with her background.

Mystery solved.

regimen

It's good to tie one on
to
make the following day
much more difficult.

Some call this
idiocy, immaturity, stupidity —

I call this
resistance training.

cam 2 cam

She's been my favorite
for some 7 years,
getting me off far too many times
to recount here.

And while she's still hot,
there has been a recent decline,
a lack of sparkle in her eyes,
a dullness in her face.

I'm afraid
the cam life is exacting its toll —

Most jobs take
far more than they give.

Mine is certainly no exception.

For this reason
I no longer show her my face.

Just
my cock.

fucked

I'm watching
an episode of *Live PD*.

Suspect pulled over,
pockets and vehicle searched.

Police find a syringe,
a baggie of meth
and a backpack full of dildos—

Poor guy.

He's fucked.

Just not
the way he had hoped.

let a stranger be your friend

I'm watching late night TV,
an ad for a suicide hotline.

Text appears on the screen:
LET A STRANGER BE YOUR FRIEND—

Ted Bundy answered phones
for a suicide hotline.

For the most part
we know how many lives he took.

But I don't guess we'll ever know
how many he saved.

permanent recall

I feel bad
for those sickened
but the outbreak
made my job much easier.

While the CDC
connected the dots
I enjoyed 2 weeks
of negligible prep work.

Our substitute,
a glorious hydroponic variety,
pre-washed/pre-chopped
for my convenience.

Unfortunately
the labor-intensive lettuce
has returned —

But unlike this Romaine
if I ever get out of here
you can bet your ass
I won't be coming back.

plop

Drunk on a Monday night
and taking a whiz
when my glasses fall from my face
right into the toilet.

I kneel, reach in, extract
and wash them
with plenty of warm water
and Irish Spring.

Perhaps
this is for the best—

My glasses
were in dire need
of a thorough cleansing.

And this
could very well improve
my piss poor outlook
on life.

Ben Newell dropped out of the Bennington Writing Seminars during his first semester, eventually resuming his studies at Spalding University where he earned an MFA. He taught high school English for one day.

www.ingramcontent.com/pod-product-compliance
Lightning Source LLC
Chambersburg PA
CBHW032218040426
42449CB00005B/651